*Beware of politicians who state that they will create 12 million jobs in 2012, especially if they state that there are 23 million people unemployed. Shouldn't they have created 23 million jobs? How did they arrive at the 12 million jobs now "number?" They could have created 12 million jobs in the last four years: they have all of the money and the connections with money (billions of dollars) to do it, but no plan. Or, was there a plan not to allow the creation of jobs coming through partnership efforts.*

*The website, www.12millionjobsnow.com has been up and operational since December 2011. Does it appear that some politicians have been "googling?" Googling here means fishing for ways to create jobs on the world wide web and stumbled upon this one and adopted for their own? <u>You be the judge.</u>*

*This program has <u>not</u> been tailored for use by politicians --- so, beware, if any politician is calling this plan his own, it is <u>fake</u>; it not heartfelt, because these politicians (and the wealthiest Americans on Wall Street and in general) could already be creating thousands and millions of jobs long before a political campaign. Why didn't they create 12 million jobs by now?*

*I'll tell you why. The strategy was to "not work across the aisle," because doing so, would have assured a second term for President Barack Obama, that's why. It is the only way that there would be a great chance to show that he is not able to work in partnership with all elected officials, that's number one. This was a well- thought out strategy; and, number two, by employing this strategy for four years, intentionally, they kept the American middle and lower classes in worse financial condition than they needed to be. Would a reasonable person believe that they really wanted to work across the aisles with President Obama but could not? This program is the one "referenced!"*

*Having worked on this night and day and day and night to develop "this blueprint, real plan with "real in-depth details" and then hearing someone shopping the idea around boldly about creating 12 million jobs without any details, I felt kicked in the stomach! They knew it was this website that inspired this statement, which has now become a "theme with no details! It left me, the author with copyright status for my intellectually property, <u>feeling intellectually raped, robbed and stabbed in the heart!</u>*

*This plan has copyright status.*

*A Book for Possibility Thinkers*

*Inspiring Author*

*George Vance McLaughlin Sr.*

## THE NEW "ARITHMETIC" JOBS CREATION PRIMER

### A Simple Way to Make Millions of New Private Sector Jobs

### Using Small Businesses as the Catalyst

**We Can Grow Our Own Jobs: Yes We Will!**

*"Ask not what your Country can do for you, but what you can do for your Country." Author: President John F. Kennedy*

*Here's One American's Creativity to Address the Nation's Number One Challenge:*

*"Creation of 12 Million New Jobs Now Americans!"*

*No Federal Dollars*
*No Politicians*
*No Outsourcing*

<u>**This is My "12 Million Jobs Now Americans" Detailed Plan**</u>
<u>**This is the Inspired by George Vance McLaughlin Methodology**</u>
<u>**& As the Senior Marketing Consultant –**</u>
<u>**It Is My Platform & I Stand On It!**</u>

# COPYRIGHT

## COPYRIGHT MATERIALS

*LegalZoom.com – Copyright© 2011*
*Registered with the Library of Congress*
*All Rights Reserved© 2012.*

---

*Copyright with LegalZoom.com (2011)*
*Website Developed December 2011*
*Book Cover (Original Artwork Completed Summer 2011)*
*Book Registered with the Library of Congress*
*Registered Non-Profit with IRS (January 2012)*
*Registered Non-Profit with State of Maryland (2012)*
*Proofreaders (Paid Consultants & Professional Editors)*
*Nearly 1,000 Persons Aware of Upcoming Publication*

DUE TO THE "NATIONAL URGENCY," THIS BOOK IS BEING RELEASED FOR SALE TO THE AMERICAN PUBLIC PRIOR TO ITS PROPOSED RELEASE DATE (AFTER REVIEW BY A PROFESSIONAL PROOFREADING & PUBLICATION COMPANY.) TO CLEAR UP ANY CONFUSION ABOUT THIS PLAN COMPARED TO ANY OTHER ONE MENTIONED BUT NOT DETAILED BY THE SAME NAME: "THE CREATION OF 12 MILLION JOBS"

# PROLOGUE

This book is "the blueprint for creating 12 million American jobs NOW!" It requires the immediate attention of all of America's visionaries, including but not limited to the following persons listed below who run and/or greatly influence large corporations and/or happen to also be billionaires and millionaires. This blueprint only needs a (1) Board of Directors, (2) Consortium of Subject-Matter Experts, (3) Chairman, and (4) both National and State-level staffing. We need America's best visionaries at the helm to implement it. Read and bring this book to the attention of (1) persons listed below, (2) persons on the most recent "Forbes Richest and Most Influential Persons List," and (3) other persons you know willing to help.

Bill and Melinda Gates      Warren Buffett        Oprah Winfrey

Donald Trump        Colon and Alma Powell        Cathy Hughes

President Bill Clinton    President Jimmy Carter    Tyler Perry

Sheila Johnson Newman    Russell Simmons      Michael Baisden

Robert L. Johnson        Steve Harvey        Rev. Jesse Jackson, Sr.

Rev. Al Sharpton      Hon. Elijah Cummings      Hon. John Lewis

E. "Magic" Johnson        Tom Joyner          Ellen Degeneres

Hon. G.K. Butterfield    Raymond C. Pierce    Lewis Brown Griggs

Forbes 100 Richest Americans: *Contact Other Influential Visionaries You Know Missing From This List (Use Social Media & Notify Them To Check This Book Out)*

# WHY EVERY AMERICAN MUST READ THIS BOOK

This book's content "highlights" will not only peak your interest but draw you into the author's reasoning, thinking and methodology for creating 12 million American jobs now without politicians, Federal dollars or outsourcing. Specifically, this book shows you how one single American unleashed the American spirit within and came up with a unique vehicle to create 12 million American jobs, right now rather than later, without need for one single Federal dollar or politician. The author gives a very descriptive detail on the "how to."

**The Business Model** is the most unique and the least expensive idea (Federal cost, $0) has NOT been brought before the American public before this book's blueprint. All it requires is the American spirit to be unleashed to go forth with all Americans working as former President Clinton called us to do: see ourselves as One America. We must work together embracing our various cultures and determine to make this world a better place by celebrating human dignity as we work to protect this "American freedom we all now have." And, the best way to do that is to "revive and grow the American economy through the creation of jobs. This national effort has no color, creed or nationality: it is an all American effort for every race, color, sex and culture: it is all inclusive. There are no different special interest groups: we are the American Jobs P-A-R-T-Y.

**The Jobs Market** is in dire shape (recession, just shy of depression) such that we must pull together and put America back in her rightful place -- economically, educationally, and scientifically -- as "Number One."

***Increasing the Resources for Small Businesses*** is the answer since they are "the key" to spark the economy and the necessary source for economic growth by the creation of jobs that are non-Federally funded; thus reducing the burden on the national debt. If we can believe it, we can achieve it ... yes, we can reduce America's debt just as President Clinton did during his presidency. We can and we must do it again. We must take the word "can't" out of our vocabulary.

***The Advertising and Marketing Strategy*** is what sets the concept above all others. Frankly, I do not know of another such concept at this time requiring no Federal dollars, no politicians, and no outsourcing while targeting small businesses to create millions of jobs and jump start the American economy. This platform is based on "the will of the people, by the people and for the people," to do the American (humanitarian) and national defense thing: save our democracy. Every generation must face up to the challenges before it: this is ours! Let's **DO SOMETHING**, let's solve this problem once and for all. This is "My Platform and I Stand On It ... Yes, I Can Create 12 Million Jobs Now." Americans with the support of all who believe it is imperative that we protect our national defense. Our economy is directly associated with our national defense: there are others who would like to see us fail and our democracy taken away from us. Freedom is not free. We can fight now and put Americans back to work, or we can do nothing and just let others run over us. I chose to believe that America is and should always be number one in the world to ensure that our democracy is maintained, our individual freedoms, and the foundation upon which this Nation was conceived: freedom for all.

1. ***Singleness of Purpose: Let's Focus America and Pull Together on This # 1 National Priority***: Just watching the news, seeing family and friends unemployed and realizing that

we narrowly escaped a depression in 2008 tells the whole jobs' market story both nationally and internationally. America must rise up and overcome these challenges. We are working our way out of a 2008 "near depression-recession." This Jobs Bill will create those jobs Americans so desperately need without costing the Federal government one dime or requiring input from politicians. They can continue to politic while we work within the infrastructure to do our part and lift ourselves from this unemployment level and move on to bigger heights than we have known before.

2. ***Financial Start-Up Costs*** will be done during the first phase of the brainstorming with the Board, Chairman and Consortium members.

# Table of Contents

COPYRIGHT .................................................................. v
PROLOGUE ................................................................. vi
WHY EVERY AMERICAN MUST READ THIS BOOK ... vii
ABOUT THE AUTHOR ...................................................... 3
INSPIRATION ............................................................... 7
DEDICATION ................................................................ 7
INTRODUCTION ........................................................... 8
BUSINESS PLAN ........................................................... 8
    Three-Point Objective: ............................................... 8
    Critical Success Factor ............................................... 9
THE JOB MARKET ........................................................ 10
    Competition .............................................................. 12
    Marketing Strategy .................................................... 13
MANAGEMENT TEAM ................................................... 14
    The Board and Subject-Matter Consortium ................. 15
    Calling on America's Best Executive Visionaries ........ 16
    Setting Up the Organization ...................................... 23
HOW TO CREATE MORE JOBS ..................................... 31
    Think Outside the Box .............................................. 31

| | |
|---|---|
| Where Else Is The Money Coming From? | 36 |
| KICK OFF | 39 |
| FISCAL ACCOUNTABILITY | 40 |
|    Accounting – Use of Coding System | 40 |
|    Use of Auditors | 42 |
| WHERE DO WE START | 43 |
| WHO TO CONTACT | 46 |
| CONCLUSION | 49 |

## ABOUT THE AUTHOR

George Vance McLaughlin, Sr. inspired the writing of this book by an independent writer using his model and hereafter referred to as "the author." .. The author's primary goal is to get America's buy-in and follow up using the concepts in this book for putting Americans back to work without the need for one Federal dollar or politician for that matter.

This book has been under development since January 2009. This concept was sent to the 2009 Presidential Inauguration Committee as one of several essays with this one addressing how to put Americans back to work at the height of the "near-recession depression." The author was seeking to win a free ticket to the 2009 Presidential Inauguration of our 44th President, Barack Obama. So, this is not a "new 2012 idea," but has been in the development stage for several years.

The essay addressed how jobs could be created and indicated that more information would be forthcoming. (Reasons prohibiting such submission can be discussed later due to actions taken against author prohibiting the submission of this information.)

Subsequently, it was put into book format for publication in 2010. Before finalizing the publication process in

2011, it was rewritten as a proposal to be put into competition where the winning proposal could get $250,000 if this proposal would be considered the best business proposal of all submitted. The entrepreneur offering this $250,000 funding grant (Michael Baisden) gave very specific criteria: (1) must have a website, (2) must be registered with IRS and State (Maryland in this case), (3) must have a well-written proposal, (4) must have business cards, (5) must have a business address, (6) must send a 3-5 minute video describing the project and (7) a number of other qualifying criteria to show that the proposal was well-documented and operational. With the deadline being December 31, 2011, we had completed the website: www.12millionjobsnow.com, gotten business cards, but not the 3-5 minute mandatory video to accompany the package.

Next, Mr. Baisden began advertising for persons to send in books and if selected, he would advertise the book on his radio show. So, I immediately went into rewriting the proposal geared directly to Mr. Baisden to help us launch the 12 million jobs program to writing "this" book to be available to the American public to also send to Mr. Baisden for consideration of being highlighted on his radio show.

Of special significance for further discussion, it is important to know all of the details from the 2009 inception of this project to its posting on the world wide web (12millionjobsnow.com) to the now release of this book in October 2012 on Amazon.com. This also is a very newsworthy story that must be told.

Again, after missing the December 31, 2011 deadline, and being inspired by George Vance McLaughlin, Sr., the ghostwriter was asked to change the information from a proposal format to a book format.

This required a great deal of work by one individual who suffered great losses and serious health concerns and had to put this book on hold. Attempts had been made to make the information public in the summer of 2011, by December 31, 2011 --- but circumstances (you need to know) halted its release each time.

Please note that this concept has nothing to do with any other commitment to create 12 million jobs. This is a platform that will be done by the American people without the Federal government involved.

<u>We need jobs and we can create them ourselves at no cost to the Federal government</u>. For others who may be announcing that they can creation 12 million new American jobs, be sure to know the differences in our plans. This book gives a clear-cut blueprint on the "how to do it as a non-politician." This one is just being shared with the American public and could not have been implemented before it became known, "how to."

Any other such commitment may be made by others who have had the opportunity to do this all along, if they knew the formula and/or proprietary information described within. If so, they would of or should have done so by now.

**INSPIRATION**

*For The George Vance McLaughlin Jobs Bill*

The George Vance McLaughlin Jobs Bill, passed unanimously by the American People on June 7, 2011, has now found its way to the American public. The book comes from the inspiration of George Vance McLaughlin, a man whose one act of helping out a neighbor in a very committed "play it forward fashion," caused many lives to be saved, touched, and enriched down through many generations.

---

**DEDICATION**

*This book is dedicated to Corey Enrique .McLaughlin, to inspire him, leaning on our Lord Jesus Christ, to help his American brothers and sisters, seek educational opportunities and gain employment, thus serving America and humanity.*

*It is also dedicated to more of the McLaughlin family: Leila, (Elmond Turner & family), George II, Leila Mae, and Mildred McLaughlin and the Gilchrist family (John, Maggie, Annie Pearl, John Robert, Spencer, Willa, Mary, Margaret, Evelyn, Maurice, Lawrence, Milton Robert Rogers and Barbara).*

## INTRODUCTION

This book shows you how one single American unleashes the American spirit within and came up with a unique vehicle to create 12 million American jobs, right now rather than later. The author gives a very descriptive detail on the "how to."

## BUSINESS PLAN

The George Vance McLaughlin Jobs Bill Act is designed to "create a vehicle to" eliminate American unemployment. It focuses on (a) making jobs for the poorest communities with the highest unemployment rates while (b) using qualifying small businesses and (c) offering tax breaks to Americans who support this Act (passed unanimously by the American people and small businesses in crises). It has a three-point objective.

### Three-Point Objective:

1. Eliminate unemployment in America
2. Focus on the poorest neighborhoods with the highest rate of unemployment
3. Make loans to small businesses to hire the unemployed, and where and when possible, recycle repayments to help create more jobs

Starting this business right away is definitely a dream come true because it allows the creation of millions of jobs to bring millions of Americans into gainful employment. The methodology in itself is a "very unique and creative vehicle" to get the job done. There are no competitors in the market place. With it being intellectual property, it can be franchised and/or imitated with the same goal in mind: the creation of millions of jobs for unemployed Americans ... NOW RATHER THAN LATER.

We know that the American job market is hurting, plain and simple. And, small businesses need a jump start to grow the American economy to get us further out of recession as soon as possible. We Americans need a brighter outlook on solving our problems. This is a positive approach to a very serious and longstanding problem: and, now our nation's biggest challenge.

**Critical Success Factor**

*I, the proposal writer inspired by George Vance McLaughlin, Sr., and the Senior Marketing Consultant, hereafter referred to as "the author" am the critical success factor* because I know how to (1) explain the concepts in very simple easy to understand terms, (2) inspire persons who can take the lead and implement this plan, (3) kick it off and (4) both motivate and inspire the masses to come onboard and get this job done RIGHT NOW! This is not the time for fault finding but picking ourselves up and moving into our future which can be brighter than our past: we determine our altitude by our attitude.

**THE JOB MARKET**

As stated in the Introduction, America needs jobs and small businesses, while most cannot afford to hire them, need more employees to spark the economic jobs growth to grow the economy. This "jobs creation blueprint" solves that problem. We can provide employees for small businesses to jump start the economy without any Federal dollars, politicians or outsourcing of American jobs outside the country.

The plight of unemployed Americans finding work is dire. Many Americans want to help their unemployed family members, neighbors and country get back to work. No ordinary everyday working Americans affected by this economic recession have had "positive and constructive" ideas brought before the American people until now. Therefore, we must accept responsibility for ourselves by:

- Deputizing ourselves to take steps to remedy this number one infrastructure problem. Our nation's number one necessity: jobs.

- Ensuring the health of **all** our citizens and the American economy

- Working together, not as the Democratic Party, the Independent Party, or the Republican Party but as the ***American Jobs Party*** where no one is left out

- Offering all to join us to work together as "One America" to face and meet the challenge to create ***12 Million Jobs NOW***, not later but RIGHT NOW!

Outside this jobs creation vehicle others have not thought up ways to do this work sooner rather than later with no Federal dollars, no outsourcing and no politicians needed.

Bottom line, there are no more Federal funds[1] for the creation of jobs for the average American citizens who are suffering greatly at the hand of decisions made by well-meaning politicians yet yielding the loss of American jobs for millions of tax paying hard working

---

[1] *Federal dollars bailed out (1) Wall Street, (2) the car industry, and made an attempt through funding the banking industry to bail out the (3) homeowners – that vote is still out if you consider the African-American community.*

Americans, many of whom are small business owners doing all they can to stay alive in today's tough market.

Now, we must bail the job industry out, and take it to higher levels of employment than America has ever seen. All things are possible, if we believe. If we believe, we can achieve, so let's get busy and roll up our sleeves.

The job market is hurting. Millions of people need jobs. Some areas have a higher unemployment rate than others, usually in African American neighborhoods as well as the poor and those living below the poverty level. This plan addresses this need for jobs in those areas targeting this market.

**Competition**

*There are no competitors*. This is a one-of-a-kind marketing strategy that has been catalogued with the Library of Congress as Intellectual Property. It is unique; however with the consent of the owner, it can be sold to entrepreneurs and become a national franchise. Just like McDonald's does cookie cutter business where they (1) sell a franchise, (2) provide uniform training, and (3) provide the products so all the owner has to do is run the business. The franchise owner have the backing of the home office to provide the administrative and product services that they need. It is a name recognition brand and the public supports it because of its name recognition. Many people can go to a local hamburger shop or they can go to McDonald's and know what they are getting, no matter what part of the country or world they are in: McDonald's burgers are the same everywhere.

This program is designed to market as many millions of products and services as American small businesses in particular, and all American businesses in general, can produce using the increased employment manpower that creating 12 million new jobs will surely provide, if we will it so beginning by getting the green light for this project.

**Marketing Strategy**

The marketing strategy is what sets the concept above all others. Frankly, I do not know of another such concept at this time requiring no Federal dollars, no politicians, and no outsourcing while utilizing small businesses to create millions of jobs and jump start the American economy. This platform is based on "the will of the people, by the people and for the people," to do the humanitarian and American thing and protect our national defense. Every generation must face up to the challenges before it: this is ours! Let's do something right now, let's solve this problem once and for all.

***This is "My Platform and I Stand On It* ...*** Yes, I Can Create 12 Million Jobs Now Americans <u>with the support of all who believe it is imperative that we restore our economy and improve our economy as one form of strengthening our national defense</u>. Our economy is directly associated with our national defense: there are others who would like to see us fail and our democracy taken away from us. Freedom is not free. We can fight now, and put Americans back to work, or we can do nothing and just let others run over us. I chose to believe that America is and should always be number one in the world to ensure that our democracy is maintained, our individual freedoms, and the foundation upon which this nation was conceived: freedom for all.

***The marketing strategy involves the creation of a management team to implement to plan's blueprint.***

MANAGEMENT TEAM

The management team will be comprised of a National Executive Board (hereafter, referred to as "the **Board**") with members who will recommend and vote on the person best suited to be the Board's **Chairman**. In addition, "subject-matter experts are vital;" therefore the Board will establish a **Consortium of Subject-Matter Experts** to help guide this jobs' creation vehicle.

Operational procedures will be developed in conformance with applicable rules and regulations governing such a non-profit" enterprise. Its goal will be to implement this plan by (1) hiring national and State-level employees to carry out the program, (2) seeking volunteers and in-kind donations, (3) ensuring that each State develops programs that meet the needs of its communities, (4) recruiting fundraisers and marketing strategists, (5) securing the assistance of successful small businesses to sit on the "Board" and give input into how to (a) evaluate and select those "applying small

---

[2] *Names are listed in the order of first names with no titles except the Presidents and First and Second Ladies: Abigail Johnson, Al Sharpton, Alice Walton, Angelina Jolie, Anne Cox Chambers, Anne Walton Kroenke, Annette Callahan, Arne Duncan, Astra Brantley, Audrey Chapman, Barbara Piasecka Johnson ,Barry Black, Benjamen Miller, Beyoncé Knowles, Bill Gates, Blair Underwood, Brad Pitts, Cathy Hughes, Charles Koch, Chris Rock, Christy Walton, Cicely Tyson, Clarence Paige, Claudia Barber, Colin Powell, Curtis James Jackson III,D L Hughley, David Koch, Debra Lee, Denzel Washington, Dick Gregory, Donald Trump, Donna Richardson, Earvin "Magic" Johnson, First Lady Michelle Obama, George Willborn, Gloria Butler, Gloria Estevan, Greg Mathis, Hillary Rodham Clinton, Iyanla Vanzant, Jada Pinkett Smith, James Carville, James Nelson, Sr., Jessie Jackson, Sr., Jim Walton, Jo Ann Linck, Joel Osteen, Joseph Simmons, Kimora Lee Simmons, Larry Ellison, Lawrence Bussey, Liliane Bettencourt, Lisa Ling, Lisa Raye, Louis Griggs, Marian Mac Millan Pictet, Martin Luther King, III, Matthew Murphy, Melinda Gates, Mya Angelou, Na'im Akbar, Nathan Butler Sr., Oprah Winfrey, Pauline Mac Millan Keinath, President Barack H. Obama, President George H. Bush, President George W. Bush, President James "Jimmy" Carter, President William "Bill" Clinton, Raymond Pierce, Robert Brantley, Roma Stewart, Rowland Martin, Russell Simmons, Russlyn Ali, Second Lady Jill Biden, Serena Williams, Sharon Murphy, Shawn Corey Carter, Shelton Jackson, Shirley Sherrod, Soledad O'Brien, Steve Harvey, T. D. Jakes, T.J. Holmes, Tina Fey, Tom Crews, Tom Hanks, Tom Joyner, Tracy Marrow, Tyler Perry, Venus Williams, Vice President Joe Biden, Wanda Sykes, Warren Buffett, Will Smith, and William Cosby.*

businesses" seeking additional funding to hire more employees and (b) how to disperse those funds through the detailed accounting and fiscal management process.

The Board and Subject-Matter Consortium

The Board will consist of outstanding American Business Owners (see 100 names of persons who will be asked to be a part of this National Initiative below)[2]. Specifically, we will ask them to share how they can best assist making this project a success based on their skills, abilities, and sphere of influence. They can begin by inspiring others in their professions and sphere of influence to participate. Also Consortium members will be asked to provide input into all areas, e.g., business, technical and program evaluation criteria so that data can be combined and presented for buy-in by keeping the President, CEO, Chairman, NEB, Consortium and the American public informed and on one accord.

Calling on America's Best Executive Visionaries

In order to convince potential investors, this organization must have a great management team to complement a great business concept. This organization must be comprised of the greatest business minds that America has to offer who have already demonstrated success in creating American jobs, marketing, advertising, network building using the state-of-the art management tools.

One criteria must be met, each person must have a burning desire to put this "unemployment fire out" receiving no monetary payments for doing so – with their love of America and desire to do his/her share to bring the economy back to number one in the world (free of charge.) Members must be visionaries who are able to think outside the box.

Americans are much more likely to invest in a Jobs Creation Program if it is headed by Americans who have name recognition and great business success, e.g., Warren Buffet, Bill and Melinda Gates, Oprah Winfrey, Donald Trump, Robert L. Johnson, Tyler Perry, the Walmart family and others.

We are seeking persons who have the demonstrated success at working hard and gaining great wealth here in America because of the many freedoms that America offers anyone to go from poverty to billionaire status: based on sheer determination, hard work and merit. This is an American goal of "if we can believe it, we can achieve it." There is no job too big for the American spirit, the American people, a combined "One America" to solve. Necessity is the mother of invention; and here we are. Let's tackle it, do it, and secure it (our economy) for the next generations to come.

It is most important that the American people buy into this "George Vance McLaughlin American Jobs Party" by believing in the financial stability of the persons working on the Management Team; then we can turn this into a "real party." There is nowhere it says that working hard to solve a problem has to be dull. Yes, we can party all the way from one job to 12 million jobs because if Mr. McLaughlin can believe it, he can achieve it with your help, prayers, and commitment to excellence in everything we do.

There is nowhere that it says that the American people must be defeated by a few people who destroyed the financial health and welfare of the masses: we get back up and become the "come back kids," being better and stronger than we were before. As Dick Gregory says, "Our greatest tool is between our ears, our brain, if we just use it " (maybe paraphrasing here.)

Board and/or Consortium members should also consist of persons who may not be well-known TV personalities or household names but are very business savvy, such as individuals who have built extraordinary successful businesses (from rags to riches who often state that only in America could this happen and welcome this opportunity to give back to those customers and communities who have supported you all of these years to help your dreams come true who are now unemployed and really need you! For example:

- Corporate leaders who want to give back

- Self-made millionaires and billionaires right here in American in the midst of our recovering from a very deep recession near depression who can offer guidance and support to struggling businesses by leading them through proven business-management practices

- Individuals making contributions from "old money family businesses and corporations"

Once created, the Board will be responsible for several things including:

1. Showing America the blueprint to be used to provide jobs based on objective criteria for selecting small businesses to financially support

2. Serving as a vehicle for the receipt of monies to make immediate jobs for the unemployed.

3. Developing a strategy to focus on the hardest area hit by the recession (Labor Statistics Dashboard and Other Socio-economic factors).

4. Serving as models by Board members contributing to the effort themselves to show their belief in its credibility and capability to make jobs immediately using the formula described within.

5. Ensuring transparency through the whole process and several mechanisms for accountability to the American people.

6. Informing Board members that they will receive no salaries; this is a humanitarian effort on behalf of those who lost their jobs. Operating expenses should come from donations, in-kind donations and volunteers. Board member should be willing to participate at his/her own expense.

7. Bringing small businesses and unemployed Americans together to provide jobs without any Federal dollars or politicians involved.

8. Restoring the American economy sooner, rather than later unleashing the American spirit to do what it does best: conceive, believe and achieve what might be impossible for some to imagine.

9. Making the McLaughlin USA Jobs Bill Act into a non-profit foundation reality.

10. Assuming financial responsibility and transparency in accordance with this vision.

Such positions that will need to be filled are, but not limited to:

1. Board of Directors
2. Chairman
3. Chief Executive Officer
4. National Marketing Consultants
5. National Program & Technology Staff
6. National Consortium of Subject-Matter Experts
7. Internal and External Independent Auditors
8. External Auditors
9. National Whistleblowers Office
10. State Directors
11. State Marketing Consultants
12. State Program & Technology Staff
13. State Consortium of Subject-Matter Experts
14. Internal State & External Independent Auditors
15. External State Auditors
16. State-Level Whistleblower Office

**Remember, we are all in this together.**

Yes, it is very hard work, but let's enjoy the ride. Hard work is good for us. Most successful people enjoy hard work and challenges. Whether we like it or not, this is ours --- to create jobs and fix a national problem. So, let's have some fun doing it. Join the USA Jobs Party (non-political); it is merely a phrase to indicate that by joining the USA Jobs Party effort, we are embracing our civic and humanitarian duties to be here for one another. And, this presents a very visible way for the Board and Consortium members to "give back" meaning show the American public just how much they appreciate the American people for our support over the many years by participating in the success of their businesses, shows, movies, music, entertainment endeavors and non-entertainment businesses. This is a great way to show your customers and fans that you "love so much and state that you fans are what matter most," just how much you love them. Fans will greatly support any entertainer or TV station that invests heavily into the McLaughlin Jobs Bill Program.

Setting Up the Organization

The "Leadership Team" volunteering to serve at the head and helm of the "George Vance McLaughlin, Sr. Jobs Party, created to make 12 million jobs will need to undertake the following to bring this project into a reality immediately:

1. Convene and determine its membership and roles.
2. Determine the city/location for its headquarters operations and seek the donation of in-kind office space, telephones, office equipment, furniture and volunteers.
3. Create a Dashboard to identify the hardest hit areas,
4. Establish a Small Business Forum to identify and qualify those small businesses in each community to participate in the program.

Simultaneously, Consortium volunteers will select both program and administrative committees on which they wish to serve, including but not limited to, the following:

1. <u>Identify the National Coordinator, Deputy National Coordinator</u> and staff to handle oversight for 50 state programs and make reports to the Chairman, Board and Subject-Area Consortium members on a regular basis.

This could be done by maintaining a Dashboard Format, where all can go to a site on the computer and see the status of any given project and priority services needed or being offered at any time via an in-depth needs assessment being conducted for each targeted area.

2. <u>Identify the 50 State Coordinators</u> (one for each state).

3. <u>Identify Volunteers for the Advertising and Marketing Team</u> comprised of the best of the best. There are people that can promote and sell just about anything. This is all for the American economy and the team will be compromised of persons who are good at advertising and marketing. In addition, if you are reading this book, you are qualified to advertise and market the concept. The Board and Consortium will work together to seek volunteers from within its group to take responsibility for this task at the National level and each State Coordinator will identify persons at the State level to assume leadership for advertising and marketing.

4. **Solicit Volunteers for an In-Kind Donations Committee** comprised of many people who know how to make contacts with schools, community centers, community business owners, non-profits, churches, and other local agencies to secure in-kind donations. Such include, but are not limited to, space at the state level for manpower training, youth training in the area of good nutrition and programs to remove this National unemployment problem by getting retirees to donate time to teach, mentor, serve as support staff to State Directors. This also includes sponsoring fundraising events approved by the State Director and the National Coordinator and Deputy Coordinator.

5. **Establish a Research and Development Committee** (brainstorming new and better ideas to keep the success rate growing faster and faster, also known as "The Research Department."

6. **Seek Volunteers for the Education Committee** comprised of interested Consortium members who "think outside the box" to get these students engaged in the learning process and demonstrated great success with teaching inner city, low income

and African American students to excel, especially where other programs have failed (for example the African American school principal who picks up his students and has a 100 percent college acceptance rate for those students in his private school); we need him and others like him onboard giving input.

7. <u>Seek Volunteers for the Arts and Sciences Committee</u> tasked with the responsibility to recommend training activities in the arts, science and technology areas to broaden the American workforce while creating new jobs simultaneously. The arts stimulate creativity (e.g., music/all kinds, theatre (skits and plays), dance/all kinds (swing dance, ball room dancing, all kinds all cultures) and such activities geared towards raising monies to create new jobs, not only meets the goal of new jobs but entertains the participants as well (a win-win). The science of food and nutrition and expected outcomes for certain diets would greatly magnify to the Americans just how important a good diet is for healthy living with the premise being if you do not have your health, you do not have anything. Your health is the most important asset you have. We must take care of our bodies. We

must equip our communities (persons of all ages) to become invested in healing ourselves physically as well as economically.

8. <u>Seek Volunteers for the Nutrition Program</u> with the responsibility to teach families how to grow their own food as well as improve their food choices for good nutrition (seeking to end childhood obesity as well as adult obesity).

9. <u>Seek Volunteers for a Mental Health (Positive "Can Do/Can Overcome" Attitude) Committee</u> to address ways to deal with the impact of fatherless homes, drug addicted parents, foster children, role of grandparents assuming the responsibility to raise their children's children as well as model programs that address this very well in certain communities (e.g., shared-community homes where a young parent lives with his/her children live and elderly persons for parenting creating a family environment where the elderly feel and are needed, necessary and important).

   a. These are group supervised home environments that work in the best interest of the parentless child and the capable elderly who can help raise the child and support his/her mother or father, whatever the case may be.

b. Most importantly, a psychological team sharing valuable information about how to overcome adversity and how to build self-esteem. This includes teaching the values that build character and teach the difference between an honest dollar compared to a dishonest dollar (the consequences) and how discipline and perseverance plays a bigger role in success than a sure role in failure when seek fast illegal money.

10. <u>Seek Volunteers for a Legal Team</u> --- yes, we need to be "lawyered up!" We should ask the Consortium members to establish a volunteer team of lawyers for this project (paid for by them, the millionaires and billionaires who can afford to give this project 10-15 lawyers, if not more, from their businesses they already own, such that the lawyers are on detail to the project, e.g., for two-three years, yet their insurance and other benefits are still paid by their current employer. This

employer can write that salary off as in-kind donation to a non-profit organization: the USA JOBS effort.

    a. For example, lawyers will draw up contracts for small business owners to sign stipulating how many jobs they will create, the job title/position and at what salary. The Board will decide whether and how the small businesses will pay the money back once they become solvent and profitable so these funds can go to another struggling small business.

    b. Another example would be that a small business would repay in other ways to give back to the community such as hiring college-bound (summer or year round) intern volunteers (no salary, just experience where the employer rates the student and provides a letter of recommendation addressing the work the student did in the community; and with partnership of a community college, this work could offer some college credit.)

11. <u>Seek Volunteers for a Business Program Evaluation Team</u> to capture baseline data for

benchmarking starting points and measuring success based on predetermined criteria (collecting ideas from the Board and Consortium to develop standardized criteria for all 50 State Directors). This team will also give input for priority focus based on ongoing needs assessments, priority areas where jobs are needed the most based on the highest rate of unemployment, particularly, but not limited to the African American communities (the hardest hit).

Operations Methodology is what makes this business model unique. There is no competition since no one is standing up to *"DO SOMETHING," independent of Federal and state dollars, politicians, and outsourcing jobs* with no out-of-pocket spending for the majority of Americans who are out of work, below the poverty level, or making less than $250,000 a year, unless they want to do so. All are welcome to participate via monetary donations or volunteering your skills and abilities to help others through this non-profit venture. This unique design of this model does not make anyone financially vulnerable while creating millions of American jobs and only those who are so led to do so should participate. This is for compassionate caring people who want to help our fellow Americans who are hurting very badly now.

By just watching the news, seeing family and friends unemployed and realizing that we narrowly escaped a depression in 2008 tells the whole jobs' market story both nationally and internationally. America must rise up and overcome these challenges. We have gone from a near depression to a recession. This Jobs Bill will create those jobs Americans so desperately need without costing the Federal government one dime or requiring input from politicians. They can continue to politic while we raise ourselves from the ashes and go on to bigger heights than we have known before.

## HOW TO CREATE MORE JOBS

### Think Outside the Box

When you read my ideas, just imagine if there were millions of us brainstorming our ideas collectively and posting them on a jobs creation website where millions can get and receive ideas about how make more employment opportunities available to all Americans seeking work.

- This non-profit will have such a website built into the fabric of the organization to capture the millions of other job creation ideas out there.

Plus, Americans reading these ideas will be inspired to create jobs in ways we cannot think of right now.

**Idea #1:** If 2,000,000 millionaires and billionaires donated $2,000,000 (two million dollars, mere pennies to them) annually <u>for three years</u> to a jobs bank to make jobs that would give us $12,000,000,000,000 to support small businesses and jump start the economy.

Further, it would give persons employed through these "commitments" the satisfaction of having at least three-years of steady employment until the economy fully recovers. This would be the millionaires and billionaires "due diligence" to keep the American economy growing after the President Bush/Vice President Cheney years of our loss of a President Clinton balanced budget with surplus. We must help one another out and this would be one way to get unemployment rates down.

Of course, there would need to be a "well-defined plan of action" about where to spend these monies and on what jobs. This would **not** be difficult for the Board to conduct a needs assessment for those cities and States with the highest unemployment rates and work with them to develop jobs to meet the needs of the community and use community resources, e.g., schools, gyms, libraries, recreational facilities as well as in-kind donations. Jobs should be geared towards the small business communities where the National and State Boards would have criteria in place for the selection of small business to receive more employees paid through the George V. McLaughlin Jobs Bill Program funds.

I believe this possible; however, there must be a vehicle and approved distribution plan in place that has the trust and the confidence of the contributors to get the job done. Therefore, I appeal to the persons listed, e.g. Warren Buffet, Bill Gates, Oprah Winfrey and other very wealthy compassionate Americans who want to put the unemployment matter behind us and move forward into reducing the American debt. This must be spearheaded by America's visionaries and proven successful business owners.

**Idea #2:** Looking at Donald Trump Program, "The Apprentice," I immediately thought, "What if these candidates were competing to see who could come up with the most creative ways to make the most jobs?" Currently, that program is geared towards which celebrity can raise the most money for his/her charity and only the winner's charity gets the money.

- I would really like to discuss this directly with Mr. Trump --- except in my vision, no one would be fired, just allow the person who creates the most jobs to be "The Winner with Runner Ups.

- Of course, any other TV stations could have their own version of this concept.

- Prize winners would not receive monetary recognition since this is an American humanitarian effort; it would spoil the originators design for such a program. This must come from the heart and a very willing spirit with great desire to help Americans for no monetary reward: none. This would weed out persons who would only "apply to help" if money is involved. If that is the case, they could have been helping all along but refused to do so because they would not be "paid for it."

- Other non-monetary winning contestant gifts that would inspire persons to seek an opportunity to be on the program could be for an opportunity to further reach their career goals, e.g., a two-year internship in an industry of his/her choice with a paid salary … so they actually work for the money.

- Have colleges and universities offer free tuition for the winner or the winner's family member (child) if the winner is responsible for creating e.g., 100-500 new American jobs.

**Idea #3:** Have business owners (millionaires and billionaires give individual donations) and have artists schedule special concerts where all proceeds go to this non-profit to put Americans back to work in those areas hardest hit with the highest unemployment rates.

- How would your customers feel or fans feel if you are making millions and billions of dollars and your name is not among those being recognized? For example, if James Brown was alive and participating, how many of his records do you believe people would go out and buy, knowing he just created 5,000 jobs with a three-year commitment? He could make movies, records, TV talk shows and other publicity opportunities with the whole American public behind him because he would be giving back and making jobs for his fellowman: Black, Brown, Red, Yellow and White based solely on America's need.

- And if John Doe had 600,000,000 customers, fans, twitter followers, but said he wanted no parts in a jobs creation program, without realizing that we walked into this recession under Bush and Cheney, we did not create it, but are charged with cleaning it up under our watch ... then how many stores that the "John Does and Mary Smiths" own would be closed by people choosing to purchase from those who support the Jobs Party effort – and not from those who oppose it.

**Idea #4**: Actors making millions of dollars per movie can give back to their fans by donating to this Board thus offering employment opportunities through small businesses in the hardest hit areas, thus giving back to the community: their fans.

**Where Else Is The Money Coming From?**

**Idea #1: Our Wealthiest Americans** -- There are many Americans who would support such a program if they had faith and trust in the persons managing the program. This is why it is crucial that those with name recognition and business excellence buy-in to this and lead the way. What about those listed as the more than 400 billionaires who reside in America ... think they want to help out? What about the hundreds of multi-millionaires, think they want to help out?

**Idea #2**: **Website Donations** Since anyone can contribute, as there are so many good-willed Americans who just have not figured out a way to help the masses of unemployed, they can contribute online and get a receipt that can be used as a taxable donation (if the Federal government or state governments allow such.)

**Idea #3:** **Public/Private Media**: What about film producers and executives making movies or a movie with all proceeds going to this Jobs Foundation with "A-List" Actors.

**Idea #4**: **Compassionate Wealthy Americans** -- There are many debt-free and otherwise successful persons making thousands of dollars, though they may not be millionaires, who may want to make sizeable donations for taxable deductions.

**Idea #5:** What about any American who just wants to donate to a jobs bank (and know where their monies ended up) and get a tax break for helping their fellow Americans? Everyone who has the heart and desire should be allowed to donate. This model focuses on identifiable individual donors to avoid any influential large corporations and businesses with ulterior motives to attempt to override the concept here.

**Idea #6:** We believe that the large influential corporations and businesses can automatically hire more employees without using this vehicle. However, we welcome large donations from any individual who happens to be associated with a large business entity.

- America always reaches out to the world in its time of crises, as we should. Do you know how many Americans really want to reach out and help ourselves, here at home, but do not have a clue on how to do it or know an organization trustworthy to donate for this purpose? This vehicle would be an option.

- Thousands of successful persons would be donating to be invited to a ceremony hosted by Vice President Biden for recognition and a handshake and a photo that shows they made jobs for Americans to pull us up out of the 2008 near-depression recession.

- People want to invest their monies with an organization that has credibility and transparency. We owe them such as well unleashing the American spirit to do what it does best: overcome all challenges and obstacles.

**KICK OFF**

Phase One begins when very successful leaders in the world of finance and business come together to work in partnership with one another to address this national crisis. Just as Bill Gates started, some months ago in 2011 or 2012, to bring a number of billionaires together to find out what charities they would be leaving their funds to in their wills (and I applaud him for doing this), so I am asking why cannot they come together to work on how many billions of dollars they can use to create American jobs now, in the dire economic time.

Financial start-up will be done during the first phase of the brainstorming with the Board's leadership team. Members consists of those who are interested in playing a vital and "immediate" role in America's economic recovery by bringing their expertise to the table, and being ready to hit the ground running.

The USA Jobs party (this plan) will <u>certainly</u> be all inclusive (no one left behind), addressing the needs of all "unemployed Americans," irrespective of race, color, national origin, sex or disability.

# FISCAL ACCOUNTABILITY

## Accounting – Use of Coding System

- Set up a coding system to identify donors, employers and employees for easy tracking of funds from receipt to the employee's payroll check such that these personally identifiable data are kept confidential. This information should be available on the worldwide web for the American people to track --- another form of citizen involvement in the process and way of "directly overseeing" any local mismanagement of funds and prohibiting fraud. What small business wants to be found guilty of mismanagement of money designed to reduce unemployment by not giving promised jobs based on the contract or loan they signed. If small businesses reach a very successful level and no longer qualify for a special loan, repayment can be dollars recycled to help others get employed.

- For example, there could be codes for each State, e.g., 01 for Alaska, for each employer, e.g., SB1, for Small Business #1 approved in the State of Alaska, a separate second code for the employer that maybe only the employer (2581) and the Board will know, and a code for the position approved, e.g., 7001 and a code for the employee selected, e.g., 1295 along with the amount of money allocated for this position ($25,000 annual for this sample purpose). Therefore, someone could look on the worldwide web and see 01S25817001129525000. The auditor will be able to use this number to decode the State, the employer, the position, the employee and the amount allotted for this position.

- In addition, an employee will have an identifier that can be used to track the employee from position to position in the event there is a problem, e.g., duplicative records showing up for more than one employer and/or position.

- Also, no employee should show up under more than one State or employer without justification that s/he may be working part-time at one place and part-time at another. For example, this would be questionable if one State reported is California and the other state reported is Florida. It would raise a red flag for further research. Also, we would not want one person having 10-20 of these jobs as a Consultant or something similar which could account for about $250,000 or $500,000 at the expense of hurting another family from getting a basic salary to survive in this very near depression "recession we are coming out from under."

**Use of Auditors**

- In addition to onboard auditor, hire independent audit agencies to track the disbursement of funds on an annual basis and report back to the Board and the public.

- Establish State-level Boards are responsible to track all monies coming into its State and be accountable for the distribution of the funds. This is another level of accountability in addition to worldwide web, audits, and the National Board's accountability.

- Text/Numeric Code: Allow persons to have a text or numeric code to donate to the non-profit.

- As a result the McLaughlin USA Jobs Board[3] should have quarterly recognition ceremonies to not only acknowledge and recognize the generous Americans who have created the most jobs through their donations, but also to give a

---

[3] *One of the first orders of business will be to seek a tax credit for those Americans who donate to this non-profit organization to create jobs for out of work Americans, many of them, their customers, clients, fans, and consumers.*

status report to the American public, including the publication of a report showing details by state and the names of donors (who seek tax breaks) and a listing of donors and amounts (who wish to remain anonymous to the American public, but known to any Federal entity that needs to know, if necessary.)

**WHERE DO WE START**

We need America's best and brightest (you) to help us brainstorm ideas to eradicate unemployment in America as well as appeal to those with the funds, power, authority and sphere of influence to create jobs to come together and begin to use a vehicle, such as this one, where we pull ourselves up by the boot straps using our own American "think-outside-the-box mentality" to dig ourselves out without the Federal government, politicians and/or outsourcing .

Necessity is the mother of invention: this is very necessary. If we can believe it, we can achieve it. We must take "can't" out of our vocabulary when it comes to reducing the national debt as full employment is a very good start.

- There is nothing that the American spirit cannot achieve once unleashed, it sees no political party

- or special interest, and it only sees healing America of whatever ails it.
- This is our nation so let's get busy taking care of our infrastructure duties as Americans: restoration of our economy to protect ourselves from possibly losing our freedom to other nations who may want to take advantage of us during this slowly easing up recession near depression.

This is the only concept on the table that can get this job done "Sooner Rather Than Later!" ***There are no competitors***; this concept can spark others to join us and/or use other creative ideas to work on this national crisis. No one has stepped up with a "Can Do Attitude!" Well, here I am … let's get busy.

Politicians cannot do everything; we are in this together, a very tough spot whether we like it or not! So, I say, let's put the rubber to the road, and show this generation that we Americans tackle big problems by turning them into opportunities to grow and find ourselves better off than before. We can exceed our wildest dreams, if we just dream and believe in that dream. What goal is more important than this one? What exactly is a goal? A goal is just a dream with a date on it. My platform is to realize the dream of 12 million jobs now Americans … now rather than later. My date is NOW!

This requires us all to work together (there is no age limit). One person can revolutionize a whole industry (for example a college student named William Gates). Yes, this is going to be hard work, but I know how to turn it into a fun project. I know how to make this work for us while we enjoy ourselves simultaneously. Who says hard work has to be dull? I disagree! Just give me an opportunity to "show what I can do . . . simply put, I can show you better than I can tell you!" Try me!

USA JOBS PARTY is very important. While we undertake this seemingly insurmountable task, we must have fun while doing so. Thus, there must be a celebratory party committee or team to bring laughter, fun, excitement and exhilaration to this national effort. The family that plays together stays together. This would include Quarterly Recognition Parties where we recognize the largest efforts being made and the most creative ones as well. As one Bishop said that makes a whole lot of sense, "It is a very poor frog that does not praise his own pond!" There are lots of things that can be done where all proceeds go to the USA JOBS PARTY to employ our fellow Americans through small businesses ... to spark the economic growth needed to save the economy. When we say Party, we mean P-A-R-T-Y, as in having lots of fun while being productive simultaneously.

## WHO TO CONTACT

Contact the billionaires and millionaires listed in this book and other you may know asking them get and read this book and help to "jump start this solution" by serving as the Chairman/Chief Executive Officer or on a National Executive Board and/or Consortium to bring this into reality and put Americans back to work now.

*PLEA FOR HELP TO GET THIS VEHICLE MOVING AND MAKING NEW JOBS FOR SMALL BUSINESSES To The Public Figures Below – Will You Support Us?*

*Jo Ann Linck             Pastor Joel Olsteen*
*Cathy Hughes            Dr. Sharon Murphy*
*U. S. Chaplain Barry Black  Lewis Brown Griggs*
*Attorney Roma Stewart    Dick Gregory*
*Russell Simmons          Magic Johnson*
*Jennifer Anniston         Sandra Bullock*
*Shawn Carter             Beyoncé Knowles Carter*
*Carmen Diaz             Kimora Lee  Simmons*
*Brad Pitt                Angelia Jolie*
*Will Smith               Jada Pinkett Smith*
*Mariah Carey             Nick Cannon*
*Tom Cruise              Billy Crystal*
*Bishop T. D. Jakes    Bishop Dr. James D. Nelson, Sr.*
*Rev. Dr. Nathan Butler, Sr.   Pastor Reginald Elliott*
*Apostle Lamont Settles       Pastor Terry Thrasher*
*Carl Snowden   Tyler Perry   Corey Franklin*
*Dr. Jamal Bryant     Pastor James D. Nelson, Jr.*
*Dr. Maya Angelou         Christine Davenport*
*Rev. Omorosa Manigault-Stallworth  Morgan Freeman*
*Diana Ross    Denzel Washington    Tracey Ellis-Ross*
*Janet Jackson             Chaka Khan*
*Minister Dr. Robert Brantley    Dr. Astra Brantley*
*Dr. Harry Olson            Dr. Na'im Akbar*
*Jack Nickolson   Dick Gregory  Spike Lee*

| | |
|---|---|
| *Michael Baisden* | *George Wilbourn* |
| *Tom Joyner* | *Steve Harvey* |
| *Blair Underwood* | *Jane Fonda* |
| *Jennifer Lopez* | *James Carville* |
| *Donald Trump* | *Colon Powell* |
| *Rev. Jesse Jackson Sr.* | *Rev. Al Sharpton* |
| *Annette Callahan* | *Rowland Martin* |
| *David Letterman* | *Jay Leno* |
| *Barbara Mikulski* | *Ellen Degeneres* |
| *Stacy Lattisaw-Jackson* | *Oprah Winfrey* |
| *Clarence Paige* | *Michael Jordan* |
| *Soledad O'Brien* | *Anderson Cooper* |
| *Kerry Washington* | *Ricky Smiley* |
| *Kirk Franklin* | *Pastor Donnie McClurkin* |
| *Lisa Raye* | *Morris Chestnut* |
| *Angela Bassett* | *Toni Braxton* |
| *Mohammad Ali* | *Laila Ali* |
| *Jill Scott* | *Patti La Belle* |
| *Elijah Cummings* | *John Lewis* |
| *Bill Gates* | *Warren Buffet* |
| *President Clinton* | *President Carter* |
| *Wil.i.am* | *Denzel Washington* |
| *G. K. Butterfield* | *Whoopi Goldberg* |

*(Americans --- Contact Other Very Successful Influential People to Help Us & Let's Get Busy)*

## CONCLUSION

This "jobs creation vehicle" has been in the development stage since 2009. Due to the serious constraints (and you deserve to know what they are), it took much longer to get this information before the American public. The substance of this "jobs creation blueprint" rather than "writing-style excellence and publication etiquette at its best" took precedence over its release due to the urgency of the information contained in this book, showing the simple "arithmetic model and straightforward way in which we Americans can take matters in our own hands and make our own jobs now working with small businesses in the communities and other community resources while being financially supported by donating and brainstorming ideas submitted to a non-profit designed to reduce the America's unemployment rate."

I trust the American public to focus on and appreciate the substantive content of this book to be so much more important than any editorial writing-style reviews.

www.ingramcontent.com/pod-product-compliance
Lightning Source LLC
Chambersburg PA
CBHW061519180526
45171CB00001B/244